SOME NOTRE DAME GREATS I'VE KNOWN

By

Andrew L. Stevans

"I applaud the work of Andrew Stevans to celebrate the fine, whole-person education provided by the Congregation of Holy Cross at its Prep Seminary ("The Little Sem") on the Notre Dame campus. Many of my colleagues in Holy Cross speak with great affection of their days there and of the committed religious who prepared them so well for life and ministry. These are stories that need to be told."

Edward A. "Monk" Malloy, C.S.C.,
President Emeritus, University of Notre Dame

Andrew L. Stevans

Some Notre Dame Greats I've Known
Excerpts from: "PREP SCHOOL DAYS, *The Seminary at The University of Notre Dame*"
© Andrew L. Stevans 2012 -2014

All Rights Reserved

ISBN: **978-0-9848340-2-0**

Library of Congress Control
Number (LCCN): **2011961681**

For Information, Contact
P.O. Box 613, Merrifield, VA 22116-0613

Printed in the USA
7290 Investment Drive, Suite B
North Charleston, SC 29418

INTRODUCTION

For some time I had hoped to find a way to "give back" to Holy Cross Seminary at Notre Dame for an excellent education that went far beyond books. Special thanks must be extended to the Holy Cross teaching Priests and Brothers, and the Sisters of Notre Dame who offered unwavering kindness, caring and understanding to all of us young men. Daily, we students were exposed to individuals "Living the Faith," and demonstrating exactly what the term meant in both the Catholic and Notre Dame traditions.

Those mentioned herein are as human and down to earth as anyone you'd meet. The stories presented are of everyday events that happened in a highly disciplined environment comprised of tough class schedules, long study halls, and grand silences--where speaking was not allowed, and your only communication was with God. What lightened the load for us seminarians were these highly dedicated individuals. They shared a quality of positive attitude and mutual concern for each of us aspirants. They remain among the giants who have inspired me.

I've been asked the question, "Why spend time in your old age writing about people, many long since deceased?" The answer is a simple one. The Priests and Sisters I met at the seminary are at the top of the mark as human beings. Each, in their unique way, has shone a great, un-diminishing light on my path through life.

Perhaps the question should be, why aren't there more of us writing about our seminary years and our Priest-leaders? I feel there is no equal to what we experienced in our attempts to be one of the chosen among the many who are called.

I dedicate this small collection of cherished memories to all seminarians who have walked with and prospered from the giants.   The author

The University of Notre Dame &
Holy Cross Seminary Grounds

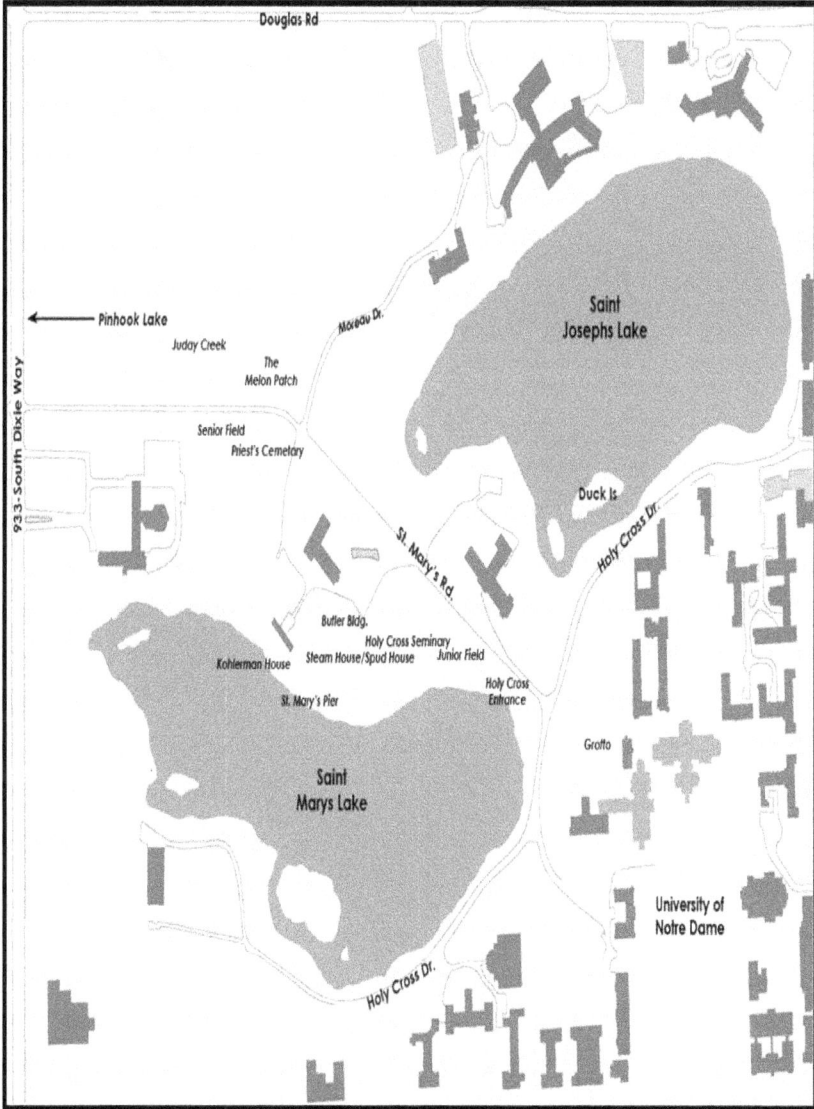

Douglas Rd

Pinhook Lake

Juday Creek

The Melon Patch

Senior Field

Priest's Cemetery

933 - South Dixie Way

Moreau Dr.

Saint Josephs Lake

Duck Is.

Holy Cross Dr.

St. Mary's Rd.

Butler Bldg.

Holy Cross Seminary

Steam House/Spud House

Junior Field

Kohlerman House

St. Mary's Pier

Holy Cross Entrance

Saint Marys Lake

Grotto

University of Notre Dame

Holy Cross Dr.

(courtesy of Michael Stevans)

THE TEACHING PRIESTS, C.S.C.
HOLY CROSS SEMINARY,
THE UNIVERSITY OF NOTRE DAME

Fr. Leonard Banas, CSC

At Holy Cross Seminary, Father Len Banas's room was located in the newly renovated quarters on the second floor of the old building. His room was directly opposite the house library, near Fathers Van Wolvlear's and O'Donnell's rooms.

I recall one afternoon, as I walked down the main corridor on the first floor, I heard quick footsteps approaching from behind. Father Banas appeared to be on a mission as he bolted up the slate steps toward the second floor, only to lose his footing halfway up.

"Dammit," he mumbled, regaining his balance..

I had cursed many times in the distant past, but this was an opportunity that couldn't be ignored. Besides, Father Banas was caught cursing in front of an impressionable, young seminarian.

"Father, what are you damning?" I asked.

Father turned toward me, almost losing his balance again.

"It's all right to damn an inanimate object," he managed to say, as he turned and continued his hectic pace up the stairs. It seemed like a perfectly logical and acceptable answer. Priests seem particularly adept at providing well grounded answers to profound philosophical inquiry. I decided there and then, I would ask Father Banas to be my senior year spiritual advisor.

On the Playing Field... The times that I saw Father Banas on the playing field were usually on weekends when we would join pick-up teams for two-hand touch football. Father would play end, possibly to watch how we executed a play; or maybe to discover any poor sportsmanship. I'm guessing.

Father Banas was a quick and agile player until he broke an ankle doing a layup shot during a basketball game on the new Butler Building's basketball court. I remember him often appearing on the court, filling the position of either referee or umpire. He shared his time with us and made us feel a part of the Holy Cross family.

Spiritual Advisor... In my senior year, I chose Father Banas as my spiritual advisor and, in my mind, as a confidant. Father's approach to spiritual direction was to act as a coach, providing his objectives for each month*. For example, one month was "Tolerance." Father provided synonyms for tolerance that were easy to relate to, such as "Charity, Mercy."

For that month I would attempt to incorporate tolerance into my daily living.

I attribute Father Banas' spiritual coaching to a list I constructed of the Seven Deadly Sins and the Seven Cardinal Virtues.

THE SEVEN DEADLY SINS
PRIDE (arrogance, pretense)
LUST (covetousness, lechery)
ANGER (wrath, rage)
GLUTTONY (indulgence, excessiveness)
USURY (greed, avarice)
ENVY (jealousy, resentfulness)
SLOTH (laziness, apathy)

THE SEVEN CARDINAL VIRTUES
VERACITY (truth, correctness)
INTEGRITY (honesty, decency)
RESPECT (reverence, esteem)
TOLERANCE (fortitude, patience)
UNDERSTANDING (judgment, insight)
EMPATHY (prudence, sensitivity)
SELF-CONTROL (temperance, restraint)

Teaching Latin… Father Banas studied classical languages at the University of Rome. We were fortunate to have him at Holy Cross for several years as an advanced Latin teacher. In my senior year, I was in one of his Latin classes. It was most fortunate (for me) that Father gave us the same semester credit question he had given a year earlier in a friend's Latin class. Father wrote "TOTI EMUL ESTO" on the board. The class was provided a clue. The inscription appeared on an ancient post in the middle of a town. Father promised extra credit for those who could explain what it said. I didn't tell Father that I knew the answer: "TO TIE MULES TO." The inscription was in English, not Latin. I received full credit.

As an aside, looking back, I'm sure "Veracity," (synonyms: "Truth, Correctness") was one of the virtues I practiced. But, when it came to advanced Latin, in a moment of weakness, I may have leaned more toward correctness than toward truth.

NOTE: Father Banas's approach to spiritual direction was similar to that presented in Ben Franklin's "Book of Virtues." Each month, Ben Franklin would select and concentrate on one of his listed 13 virtues as character building exercises, practicing Humility or Moderation or Sincerity—and thus growing his personal character a little at a time.

Fr. William Brinker, CSC

Father Bill Brinker had resided at Holy Cross several years before my class arrived. Father was a Religion, Math and Physics instructor. I had Father Brinker for a Physics 101 class.

I remember my first meeting with Father Brinker. It was during my sophomore year. He ran the supplies store at Holy Cross. The store carried school supplies but also sold chewing gum and candy bars. I was an occasional visitor, leveraging the money earned during my summer months at home. I purchased only the largest, and therefore the longest lasting candy bars. Later, during that year, I discovered the U.S. Mail laundry service. If I sent my laundry home, mom would deposit candy and other snacks buried beneath the clean, folded clothing thus allowing me to reserve my scant savings for other urgent purchases.

Upon meeting Father Brinker, I immediately identified with him. He reminded me of my father. Though 12 years younger than dad, Father Brinker had the same lanky build and a certain body language that, combined with a matter-of-fact way of speaking, if he and dad were observed talking together, one might suspect they were brothers.

Like all resident Priests at Holy Cross, I had only strong support from Father Brinker, never a harsh word or reprimand—though I can think of a few times when, in Father Brinker's situation, dad would have barked a few abrupt commands.

Part of the Holy Cross line-up
Back Row: Dick Kovalik, Don Kaiser, Jon Lullo, Jim Keating
Front Row: Rog Sowala, Cy Speltz, Mike Wilsey, Mike Gelven, Ed Whalen

Father Brinker's Baseball team... Father Brinker often played or coached Holy Cross sports. With Father

Fiedler's help, Father Brinker decided to organize and coach a house baseball team.

It was in the spring of our junior year when the two Priests, both experienced athletes, began putting together a Holy Cross baseball team. We met daily, and began a Priest-directed series of practices geared toward building an unbeatable batting and fielding capability.

Their approach was simple. Father Brinker, backed by Father Fiedler coached each position, providing us the expertise of their many years of playing experience. I played third base. Under the Priests' watchful eye, I fielded grounders and learned how to throw quickly to first base by stepping forward and spinning off my left foot.

During baseball practices, when I felt frustrated, having to repeat multiple throws from third to first base in order to meet Father Brinker's strict standard, there was always encouragement and his recommended new way to "try it again." After a short while and much practice retrieving grounders thrown by Father Fiedler, and observed by Father Brinker, they were satisfied that my left arm snag and strong, right arm throw to first base would not end up out in right field some of the time. After several more practices I found I was able to throw third to first from any standing position, even side-arming some of my throws accurately.

After satisfying our coaches that we were the best we could ever be, the Holy Cross house team acquired Notre Dame uniforms. The intense practices had paid off with easy wins against other Holy Cross teams. The house team became known as *Father Brinker's baseball team.*

In an initial game, we were invited to play Moreau house, the college equivalent of Holy Cross. Neither Priest coach attended the game. It was a cold day in May, with snow flurries in the air. We looked impressive in our Notre Dame uniforms. Holy Cross offered some strong competition, but lost the game to Moreau. It was chalked up as a loss to an older and more experienced team.

A few weeks after the loss to Moreau Father Brinker learned that Sacred Heart Preparatory Seminary in Donaldson Indiana had a good baseball team. We were invited to Sacred Heart for a game. Since it was late in the spring, this game would be our last before the summer break.

After an hour bus ride down the Liberty Highway, Holy Cross arrived at Sacred Heart. Upon disembarking from the bus, it was obvious to everyone where we were from. The words "Notre Dame" were emblazoned across the fronts of our uniforms.

The opposing Sacred Heart team appeared in street clothes. Their pitcher was nondescript, tall and thin, on the gangly side, and a bit slow in delivery during his warm up. The game began.

To this day, I can remember the "WOP!" of the delivery as each fast ball hit the catcher's mitt.

"You're out!" resounded after our Holy Cross players went through their at-plate exercise. It didn't matter the batting order, or the substitutes or Father Brinker's coaching; we simply couldn't hit off this Sacred Heart pitcher. His ability to sustain a fast ball delivery for many innings was a wake-up call for our team.

Cy Speltz, our experienced pitcher, had a consistent delivery that had won Holy Cross many games. We suffered through hit after hit from the Sacred Heart batters. When not talking to the Priests from Sacred Heart, Father Brinker was busy rallying our team.

During one of the later innings, with Holy Cross at bat and two out, I managed to connect with the ball. It was a solid line drive down the third base line almost hitting Sacred Heart's third baseman. The ball continued into left field. I made it to first base or second with Keating advancing to third after stealing second earlier. It didn't really matter. We struck out again.

The Holy Cross/Notre Dame uniforms no longer looked as new as they had just a short time earlier. I remember Keating's looking as though he had slid into all four bases on his stomach. We lost that game as well. Following the loss, Father Brinker was conciliatory with positive remarks about some of our key plays. But we knew his true feelings by his silence on the return trip to Holy Cross.

Father Bill Brinker, rallying Holy Cross (standing, far left, hand on his knee)

Remembering Father Brinker's Physics Class...

Holy Cross Seniors had shared rooms on the second and third floors of the old building. Tom Norris and Jon Lullo shared a room directly across the hall from Andy Roering's and my room. Both of the rooms were located at the end of the third floor hall looking out toward St. Mary's Lake, Notre Dame's Golden Dome and Sacred Heart Church.

Norris's morning assignment was to awaken the house by ringing a large brass bell. One ding at each room, multiple dings at each of the dorms. I secretly envied both Norris' and Lullo's ability with studies but decided early on not to bother them or some of my other classmates with my minutia, namely, Father Brinker's difficult physics assignments.

I often had tall hurdles to jump when it came to solving physics problems. I recall some frustration with the algebraic equations for converting Fahrenheit to Centigrade and Centigrade to Fahrenheit.

This one particular morning, Norris had already awakened us and was on his way to awaken the student dorms. Lullo exited his room and was moving fast when I asked if he had solved the previous day's physics assignment. We were on a grand silence until breakfast, but I was feeling a growing desperation. Lullo looked at my open physics book and quickly scanned the assignment.

"Ah, no. Sorry. I'm going to work on that later this morning." Lullo continued at his quick pace down the hall.

I had always classified Lullo and a few other classmates as math whizzes. Physics' algebraic equations should have been a snap for either of them. On the other hand, due to poor study habits, I had barely passed first year algebra at St. James, back in Pittsburgh. I could only blame myself. I stood in the hall for a moment, half hoping that Lullo would turn and say,

"Oh, yeah. I remember now…"

It didn't happen.

I waited for Norris to return from bell ringing to ask his help in solving the problem. I finally concluded that he had gone directly to chapel. I too attended chapel and, while I was kneeling during Mass, I was able to scratch possible solutions on the top railing of the chapel seat in front of me. I had learned during a difficult sophomore Geometry class that the markings easily erased. I started over many times.

It then occurred to me that the steam room had a outdoor thermometer that provided both Fahrenheit and Centigrade readings at any given temperature. Following chapel and breakfast, I took the physics book to the steam room, fed coal to satisfy the hungry furnace, then spent the next 30 minutes sitting on the cold basement steam-room steps, substituting values in the two equations until the answers matched the outdoor thermometer readings. For a brief period of time, I felt I was a tiny bit ahead of the ball in Father Brinker's Physics class.

Fr. Joseph "Harry" Fiedler, CSC

If you can imagine a strong, disciplined, no-nonsense, unpretentious Priest, who often hid his kind and caring side, you're most likely thinking of Father Joseph "Harry" Fiedler. It wasn't long after my sophomore classmates arrived at Holy Cross that I was summoned by Father Fiedler. I had already heard about Father Fiedler's interest in sports, his natural athletic ability, and the rumor of an earlier association with a Chicago White Sox farm team.

I also knew Father Fiedler had a hearing problem and allowed myself to be entertained by students describing the results of whispering in Latin class to answer Father's question. When Father adjusted his hearing aid volume the student would talk normally causing Father to quickly turn down the volume. I also knew that Father Fiedler was the director of studies at Holy Cross.

As I entered the room, Father was right to the point, "Mr. Stevans, you'll have to select a Priest as a spiritual advisor as soon as possible. Also, I want you to retake first year Latin."

"Yes Father. Well, would you be my spiritual advisor?" It was a spontaneous request, since I'd come unprepared.

"Of course I will. Thanks for stopping by."

That was it. I left the room and continued down to the sophomore locker room to find out what a spiritual advisor was, and what I had just committed to. I learned that a spiritual advisor offers spiritual guidance and support—the "go to" person.

I soon decided that I couldn't go wrong with Father Fiedler as my spiritual advisor since he was a supportive director of studies. Even though he came across as a no nonsense kind of guy, I tried on several occasions to engage Father in friendly conversation. I once asked why he had a large trunk at the foot of his bed. It was obviously meticulously maintained, shiny black with ornamental hinges and a sophisticated metal design across the top. It appeared to be his sole possession. The rest of his room was Spartan, containing a small bed, a lighted desk, and a closet on the far side of the room. The floor had no rug.

I had hoped for an entertaining anecdote, perhaps about the trunk traveling across Europe with an aunt who presented it to him years earlier. This actually happened to my oldest brother, Jack, who inherited his trunk from a great aunt.

Father was dismissive about it, but quick to comment that soon I would be asked to take a vow of poverty as he had. He launched into a short lecture on the priesthood and poverty.

For me, geometry would be that year's nemesis. It came to pass, as the sophomore year flew by, that I'd often find myself with a frustrating, unsolvable geometry problem. The problem seemed to have little supportive proof from the list of axioms and corollaries that made up geometry. I would reluctantly join the line of other frustrated students at Father Fiedler's door, seeking his learned advice. He never failed me.

A natural in sports... In pick-up games of two-hand-touch football, or on the basketball court, Father Fiedler would often join in. He was in his early 50's and a large man, but agile for his size. His hands were immense. I imagined him pounding in fence posts on the family farm, or catching a line drive without effort. His hands had obviously done heavy labor.

A class mate, Skinner, an avid hand ball player, mentioned Father Fiedler's skill on the handball court. With apparent ease he could move and change direction quickly and often won. It was obvious that Father enjoyed sports, and could easily compete against much younger men on the playing field, as well as on the basketball and handball courts.

Of the many times I visited Father Fiedler's room, burdened with math, Latin or other school problems, or to discuss a personal problem and obtain guidance from him as my spiritual advisor, I never again raised a question about the trunk, though I admired it from afar. I was afraid to ask what he had in the closet.

Father's Lumberjacks... One day, following a football game, Father Fiedler approached me near the junior field. In addition to being the director of studies, Father was also in charge of the Holy Cross grounds. He asked if I'd like to cut up some large, felled trees lying near the junior playing field.

"I need to get those trees cut into manageable sizes to load in a truck and haul off the property. I have some heavy-duty wedges, a couple of sledgehammers and a two-man saw. Are you interested?" Father already knew I'd be receptive to any kind of physical activity, but I had to find someone as interested as I was to be my other half on the two-man saw. Klouda might be interested, I thought. He seemed anxious to build up his too tall somewhat thin physique.

"Yes, Father, and I think Klouda might be interested too. I'll check with him. When do you want us to start?"

"Could you get started tomorrow, after your football game? Remember, this is a commitment of at least several weeks, and there are other trees that I can have felled. You can cut those up as well."

"Father, they're fairly large trees."

"Yes, they average 3 to 4 feet across. That's why you'll need a two-man saw, some wedges and a sledge hammer." Father said. I became excited about lumbering more than I let on. I knew Klouda would be as well.

The next day, after our two-hand touch football games, Klouda and I met Father Fiedler at Herman's Tool shed.

"Make sure to store the tools in the shed each day, after you're finished."

"Yes, Father."

As we exited the shed Father pointed to a small garden near the Sisters' quarters. "And make sure you don't trample the flowers when entering or exiting the shed with the tools." Father smiled. "I planted them and nurtured them, but the Sisters would be unforgiving if they were damaged."

"Yes Father. Thank you."

Klouda and I looked at each other with un-erasable smiles. What a racket we had fallen into. We would emerge fit as lumberjacks and have some enjoyment while doing it.

We became dedicated to the tree-cutting job. It lasted throughout the fall, and it wasn't long before Klouda put on several pounds and developed a swagger. My football team's quarterback started calling me "Pierre." The nickname stuck.

Latin Request... Late in my junior year, Father Fiedler approached me.

"Mr. Counihan is struggling with his Latin. Can you take some time and review what he knows and what he doesn't know." Father didn't order me, but simply asked if I could help a fellow student.

"Father, I'll try."

I also had trouble with first year Latin, but later, when advanced Latin class was combined with first-year French--a language related to Latin—things seemed to fall into place.

For an hour after dinner each evening, Bob Counihan and I met in one of the classrooms at the Butler Building. Initially we talked about parts of speech in English. Then, using his Latin book we reviewed declensions and conjugations, cum clauses, and so forth. On the board I demonstrated how various parts of speech fit together and relied on one another in Latin sentences.

In addition to reviewing English to Latin translations in Counihan's Latin book, occasionally, we studied sentence structure and endings in the Daily Missal, in preparation for the following day's Latin Mass. Counihan showed a genuine interest in this approach and his understanding grew rapidly.

I'm sure that my satisfaction—and fascination--from seeing a student learn a subject following my directions, far outweighed Counihan's satisfaction with learning.

Father Fiedler had launched me on a teaching quest I would follow for most of my adult life.

11 years Later... During the summer of 1966, I called Holy Cross from a local hotel. I had been visiting the Midwest with my wife and two young children. Father Bill Simmons answered the phone and was surprised to hear from me. I asked Father if I could stop by with the family to visit with Father Fiedler and several of my former classmates, who were now ordained Priests.

As we drove down St. Mary's road, I noticed some newly planted trees, near the lake on the Holy Cross grounds. Everything else appeared pretty much as I had remembered.

As we approached the north side of the Holy Cross, Fr. Fiedler was there, grinning and waving to us. Several seminarians were laughing with Father but dismissed themselves as we parked.

I introduced the family. The first thing I noticed differently about Father Fiedler was his ability to hear everything I was saying. He explained his new hearing aid was far better than the old one. He considered his hearing near 100%. Father proceeded to give us a short walking tour of the grounds, introducing us to several of the resident Priests. They all appeared to be around my age.

Father and I discussed my life's journey to date—the Navy, my trip to Rome, my education and marriage, even the recent purchase of the Old School House in North Greece, New York, a historic site, that he seemed particularly interested in. We discussed briefly the baptism of my children and a young CSC Priest in North Greece, temporarily assigned to the local Catholic parish. Apparently, Father also had heard the rumor that my sophomore class had stolen melons from Brother Seraphim's melon patch a dozen years earlier. Smiling, he asked if there was any credence to the rumor. I said that I had heard the same rumor. We both laughed.

I really wanted to talk about my classmates and what Father knew of their lives. It turned out Father had bits and pieces of information but was obviously fully absorbed with the current batch of young candidates for the priesthood. We both began reminiscing about sports and unforgettable wins. Father said he still continued to play some handball and pick-up football. As we talked outside the building, near the freshman/sophomore locker rooms more than one seminarian spoke to Father, and engaged him in conversation, a few times out of earshot. I truly felt like I'd returned home to the family of Holy Cross. Father excused himself to try to phone my classmates. I learned later they were playing golf and couldn't be reached.

On Father Fiedler's return, he had a surprise. Fathers Pete Sandonato and Jerry Knoll had joined Father Fiedler to welcome us. Both Priests took an interest in Dale, our oldest son, who was four at the time. I assured the Fathers that Dale was interested in everything that his dad had done at Holy Cross, including (and in particular) fishing St. Mary's Lake.

Much too soon, the Priests had to excuse themselves. After receiving Father Fiedler's blessing, I drove out to the edge of the Holy Cross property and Brother Seraphim's old melon patch. I related a kid friendly version of us seminarians stealing melons from the melon patch. Dale understood all too well, and asked when we were going to eat.

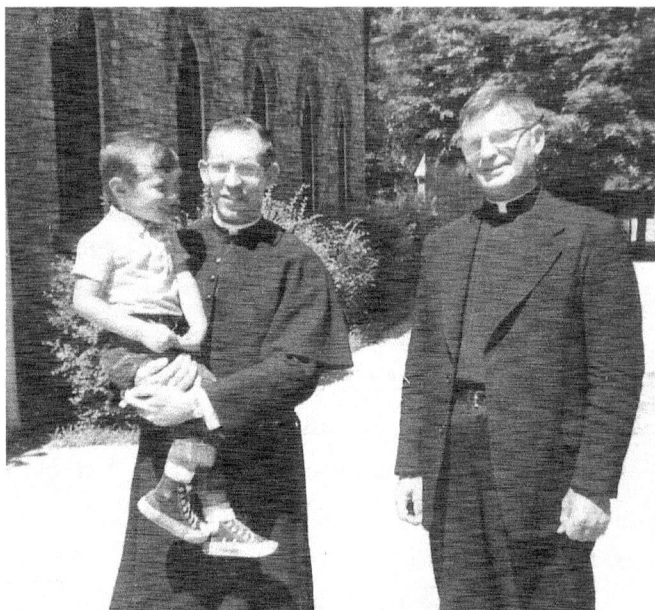

1966: Son Dale, Fr. Knoll & Fr. Fiedler
The above photo was taken just months before the
closing of Holy Cross Seminary

Fr. Nicholas Langenderfer, CSC

Back in 1954, I met Father Nick Langenderfer. Our meeting was a most urgent one. Following a summer vacation at home in Pittsburgh, I had returned to Holy Cross Seminary at The University of Notre Dame to begin my junior year. School tradition required we play a Junior-Senior touch football game. During the game, I suffered a knee injury that over-night had swollen considerably. I was in extreme pain. It was almost impossible to walk.

I finally staggered to Father Langenderfer's room, located just outside the junior dorm. Father was relatively new to Holy Cross but I had seen him enter his room the night before. "Father, I need help," is all I recall saying.

Father Langenderfer was of medium build and tanned. He wore large glasses that made his face look somewhat thinner. Although Father appeared initially to have a reserved manner, he immediately helped me back to bed and summoned Father Fiedler from the refectory and Sr. St Rita from the infirmary. I was then transported to the Notre Dame infirmary. A week later I was taken to St. Joe Hospital where the knee was drained. I returned to Holy Cross on crutches.

Though Fr. Langenderfer taught classes at Holy Cross in 1954 and 1955, I do not recall encountering him again, either during my junior or senior years. It's possible that he moved out of Holy Cross to one of the Notre Dame Halls, nearby. I also do not recall thanking him for his help in sizing up my medical situation and his quick follow-through. But Father did remain in my memory. Over the years I wondered what became of this quiet, reserved gentleman.

I contacted Notre Dame's Holy Cross Province archives seeking information on Father and discovered that Nick Langenderfer was the 14th child (and a twin) four boys and 10 girls, of a devout Ohio Catholic family. He was president of his high school senior class.

Though he was 17 years ahead of me, he and I shared several uncanny parallels in our lives. He had a love of competitive sports and played football, basketball and baseball in high school (mine at Holy Cross Seminary). After high school we both joined the Navy. Following our Navy enlistments, we both worked for oil companies (Sun Oil, Ohio) and (Gulf Oil, Pittsburgh). We both applied for Navy Flight School. He was accepted; I failed the eye exam (color blindness). At this point our lives went separate ways, he to

Notre Dame and the Priesthood and I to Penn State and married life.

During his flight training in Iowa, Nick Langenderfer was a pitcher for the Iowa Seahawks (University of Iowa). At the age of 26, he arrived at Notre Dame to request acceptance into the Priesthood. He graduated from Notre Dame in 1950 and was ordained a Priest in 1954. Father Langenderfer, CSC's first assignment was as an instructor at Holy Cross Seminary, where he arrived just in time to assist me with my injured knee.

In 1961, at age 41, Father Langenderfer became Superior of Holy Cross Seminary, a position he maintained for four years (1961 – 1964).

> *It was during his tenure at Holy Cross that one of his sisters (fourth eldest: Hilda Langenderfer) from his large Ohio family, Sr. Mary Anselm, S.N.D., was appointed Superior General/Rome of the Sisters of Notre Dame (1962 – 1974).*

Following his position as Holy Cross Superior, Father Langenderfer became Superior of Notre Dame High School in Niles, Illinois (1967-1973).

What a memorable career Fr. Langenderfer had! Even his pastoral-care appointments were exceptional: Director of the Fatima Retreat Center at Notre Dame (1965-1967); Assistant Pastor then Pastor of St. Bernard's Parish in Watertown, WI (1973-1978); Pastor of St. Francis Xavier Parish in Burbank, CA (1978-1985) and, in 1985, appointed Chaplain, St. Mary's Convent at Notre Dame, until his retirement in 1986 at Holy Cross Retirement House at Notre Dame. This gifted man, the youngest brother of 13 siblings, died on Sunday, July 28, 1986.

Had I known Father Langenderfer was at Fatima Retreat House when I visited Holy Cross in 1966 with my wife and two children, I would definitely have stopped by. I could have visited with him—and given him a belated thank you. I'm sure the "sea stories" of our Navy escapades would have allowed us to entertain each other for hours.

Although we both led full and rewarding lives, I wish I had known Father Langenderfer better. I wish we had become good friends.

Fr. Lawrence LeVasseur, CSC

During my years at Holy Cross, Father Larry LeVasseur was assistant superior. Father became Holy Cross superior three years following my graduation.

The Race... During the spring of our junior year, Father LeVasseur, originally from *slow* New Orleans, increased his fame and gained our respect for his sportsmanship, when he took up a speedy sophomore's, Henry Reyes, dare to "try to catch him" in a 100 yard dash.

Like most of us, Father LeVasseur probably knew or had witnessed a few things about Reyes that, I'm pretty sure, made him think twice about a short-distance race with this upstart Texan. First, Reyes was undoubtedly fast and maneuverable, able to change direction at full speed during his many football carries on the junior field turf. Second, Reyes was, at heart, a die-hard Longhorn football fan, willing to

35

compete against any Notre Damer to prove his loyalty—to the Longhorns.

At Holy Cross, Father LeVasseur came across as quick thinking but easy-going. He spoke in a low monotone, adding to his laid-back image. Father LeVasseur was a matter-of-fact, attentive assistant superior who, according to some, had developed a slight paunch while working in the seminary's candy and supplies store. Though worth mentioning, it was simply a rumor, most likely unfounded since Father did react positively to Reyes' challenge. Yet, I didn't see Father on the playing fields as much as, for example, Father O'Donnell or Father Fiedler, so this lent to the intrigue.

Actually, many of us were surprised when Father LeVasseur took Reyes up on his offer. Without ceremony, in the middle of the week, just before the lunch bell rang, the two runners lined up on St. Mary's Road, near St. Joe House. Of course the student body was aware of everything and watched from the grounds of Holy Cross, from the many refectory windows, and from several second floor classrooms.

The race began. I don't recall Father bothering to remove his cassock—he may have hitched it up and tucked it into his belt on one side. The two were well matched except for the 15 year age difference. Both Reyes and Father LeVasseur were under six feet. Both were fast. During the race, Reyes was using his full body and flailing arms trying to widen the gap between himself and Father. Meanwhile, Father LeVasseur appeared focused, like a sprinter, not paying attention to Reyes or to any of us cheering them on. Father's eyes stared directly ahead. His arms moved methodically with his quick body movements. Initially, his strides were a slight chopping motion, but smoothed as he gained speed during the 100 meter sprint.

As best as we could determine, Father LeVasseur won by a half stride. There was much discussion about this. Reyes claimed he was ahead most of the way, and that should count for something. But the conclusion among classmates was that Father LeVasseur had won the race. The afternoon lunch discussion was all about foot races, and the great 100 meter Olympics winners including Jesse "J.C." Owens, with four gold medals, and other Olympic runners. For a brief time, following the Reyes/Fr. LeVasseur race, there were challenges made among Holy Cross students and races run around St. Mary's Lake's one-mile perimeter, and even around the longer St Joe's Lake. Father LeVasseur did not comment on his win.

Dozing in Apologetics Class... As clearly as I can remember, Apologetics was a theology course devoted to the proofs of the existence of God and the divine origin and authority of Christianity. I don't think you'll find this definition elsewhere.

In our senior year, fall semester, we were required to take the course in apologetics. It was taught by Father LeVasseur. Unfortunately, the course was scheduled at 4:00 p.m., the last class of the day. From day one, it was obvious that Father would teach in the same deep monotone he used when saying morning Mass. To most of the class, the course was not an exciting subject, ranking right up there with "The

History of Mankind," and, in my case, Father Simmons' Greek 101 class.

My concern was about the promised tests Father LeVasseur administered from time-to-time—I think he called them "snap quizzes." I listened and I studied. The monotone was sleep defying. As hard as I tried, I caught myself dosing off as though in response to hypnotic suggestion.

Occasionally, Father's voice lifted a note or two, or his voice became louder, emphasizing a current discussion subject. Unfortunately, a large part of his approach to teaching was to read from the book. This mattered little, since Father's reading voice was as monotone as his discussion voice.

I can't explain why I still remember core subject material taught in Father LeVasseur's Apologetics class. During that same semester, I read and relished the complete volumes of Milton's "Paradise Lost" and "Paradise Regained." Today, I remember nothing of these great works—not a single stanza! Yet, when Father LeVasseur presented the Cosmological and the Teleological Arguments* as proof of the existence of God, the facts became imbedded, forever, somewhere in my subconscious mind. I can only conclude that, in spite of my complaints about his hypnotizing, sleep inducing monotone, Father LeVasseur was a gifted teacher.

Two proofs for the existence of God: the Cosmological and the Teleological Arguments. The first, involved the intelligent organization of the universe, the second, the order of the seasons, the cycles of plant life, as well as the cycles of all living things on earth.

Fr. William "Tam" Lyons, C.S.C.

One of our older resident Priests at Holy Cross, Father Lyons, taught history for many years at Notre Dame, and to most of us at Holy Cross. Frequently, Father could be found in the Holy Cross library either reading a book--sometimes he would leaf through books while standing--or selecting a number of books to take with him for later reading consumption. I attended Father Lyons History class when many of our classes were still held at Holy Cross House, not at the new Butler Building. I don't recall much that was taught. I think Father knew History wasn't the most exciting subject for some of us.

When he mentioned the great navigators and explorers of the pre and post Columbus period, he frequently raised his voice and with a dramatic flourish, much like a stage actor setting a scene, would enliven his lectures.

"Sniff the sea breezes with Ferdinand Magellan, as he and his five ships sail across the Pacific!" or, "Join the Canadian explorer, Louis Joliet, as he explores the Great Lakes and discovers the Mississippi River!"

Walking Exercise... Father Lyons was in his mid-60's, of average, perhaps even small build, white haired and under six feet tall. A dedicated walker during all the time we knew him, Father carried a walking stick, sometimes a cane. While playing football or baseball on the senior playing field, we often saw Father walking out St. Mary's Road. At other times he'd take a quick stroll around St. Joe Lake, or be seen walking quickly up from the Holy Cross entrance, returning from a jaunt on Notre Dame's main campus.

One day Father returned to Holy Cross from the direction of Moreau Seminary, walking quickly past the new Butler Building. It was a crisp fall day and I noticed steam when he exhaled, indicating to me that he'd most likely completed one of his hikes.

As he approached, he stopped for a moment to tie his shoe, lowering his knee to the ground. Through his black slacks, I noticed the outline of large, developed leg muscles and realized how powerfully built he was. He walked by, nodded and smiled to us as he often did, and entered Holy Cross through the senior recreation room door, where there were steps to the upper floors and the Priest quarters.

It was about mid semester when I realized Father raised his voice and spoke in flowery prose to awaken a classmate who was nodding off. I was one of them.

Fr. William McAuliffe, CSC

During our years at Holy Cross Seminary, Father William McAuliffe, a larger then life, multi-talented Priest, assumed the role of Gregorian chant choir director at Moreau and later, at Holy Cross. Father made himself available for one-hour each week to teach from the Liber Usualis, a few thousand page treasury of Catholic Gregorian chants, compiled over the years by the monks at the Abbey of Solesmes in France.

Punctuality and Perfection... Father McAuliffe arrived at the Holy Cross chapel punctually, at 7:00 p.m, and expected each of us to be ready for a hands-on Gregorian music practice. In addition to his presumption that we already knew the several psalms that made up the basis for much of the Gregorian chant, Father assumed we were well versed in reading music.

"It's DO-ME-LA-DO, not DO-ME-SOL-DO. Let's do it again."

One evening Kaiser, a junior, arrived late for the one-hour session. He attempted to slip into an aisle at the back of the chapel.

"No, no, you come up here. If you're going to disturb us, you may as well do it right. Now, sit in the first row."

Father was a perfectionist when it came to Latin diction, allocution and accent. We each had a house copy of the Liber Usualis and were expected to use it. An extreme incident happened when one of the Mullen brothers forgot to open his Liber Usualis and pay attention. This quickly brought down the Father McAuliffe wrath. In an instant a Liber Usualis was flying through the air toward the front pews. According to one account, Mullen ducked. There was a sudden quiet in the chapel.

Father McAuliffe, a Step Forward... In post Vatican II years, Father McAuliffe embarked on a more demanding mission, emerging as a exceptional lecturer and demonstrating a great love of parish ministry.

Several years after our class graduation, Fathers Charles Callahan and Richard Grimm established the *Holy Cross Associate Family* comprised of parents, family and friends of Holy Cross religious and seminarians. This effort was an extension of the *Holy Cross Lay Family groups* around the country. For many years, my father headed the Pittsburgh, PA chapter.

Father McAuliffe became involved during the building of the new Moreau Seminary. He transformed the *Holy Cross Associate Family* into the *Holy Cross Association* with a focus on direct mail support for the operational needs of both Moreau Seminary and Holy Cross Seminary. My eldest brother, Jack, headed up the Pittsburgh, PA group for several years. The Holy Cross Association's direct mail program was unique primarily due to Father McAuliffe's pastoral and individual outreach to each name on the mailing list.

Being a perfectionist in all he attempted, the effort was first class and the patron participation reached many thousands of families.

Recalling the More Exciting, Earlier Years… Yet, during our seminary days and Father's less mellow years, we vividly remember the "Canadian Goose incident"—some of us think it may have been a Canadian goose using St. Mary's Lake as a rest stop. Father was suddenly attacked by the large bird. Father raised his brief case to protect himself, finally throwing the brief case at the disturbed bird. The brief case handle broke and the brief case ended up in the lake, floating away from the shore line, sheets of music floating on the water. Father McAuliffe, with his cassock tucked in his belt, and a fallen tree limb in his hand, waded into the water halfway up his pant legs to finally reach and retrieve some of the sheet music. The brief case sank to the bottom of the lake.

During our senior year at Holy Cross, Father McAuliffe was assigned as disciplinarian (Prefect of Discipline) at Notre Dame. One evening, following a Notre Dame-Michigan football game (Michigan lost), Father found two Michigan football players wandering around campus, possibly looking for trouble. He confronted them and one took a swing at him--not a smart thing to do to anyone, and certainly not to a Priest on a Catholic University campus. Being a former athlete with good reflexes, Father McAuliffe ducked late and sustained bruises to his face. The incident was quickly brought under control. The "former" Michigan players returned to face charges.

To this day we discuss incidents involving Father McAuliffe. We do believe this enigmatic man was a true man of God.

Fr. Dean O'Donnell, CSC

Father Dean O'Donnell—we called him "Father O'D"-- taught English and resided at Holy Cross year 'round. His teaching style was low-key, and laid back.

Upon his arrival at English class, you could count on a cheerful "Hello folks," Father's daily greeting. At every class I attended, Father appeared upbeat. He lit up the room with his presence.

Frequently, Father selected class essays that he read out loud, and then asked the class for constructive criticism. I remember once when my turn came up. The essay described Conroy's Funeral Home, back in my home town near Pittsburgh. I had used the word "wainscoting" to describe the wood paneling in the funeral home. Apparently, over the years, between Pittsburgh and the mid-west, the term had been lost. No one seemed to know what wainscoting was, and a few members of the class finally admitted they thought the essay was copied. The comments came as a shock to Father O'D, and particularly to me. These were my close buddies for three years. What had I done to deserve the comment?

Father quickly corrected the naysayers, explaining that he had been reading my essays for awhile and this was definitely my work. I felt proud. He further assured the class there were many of my old mistakes appearing in the essay. I have seldom felt my ego inflated and deflated so quickly.

In our junior year, Father O'D had everyone memorize two of several passages he had selected from Shakespeare's writing. To this day I can recall most of Marullus's speech,

"You rocks, you stones,
You worse than senseless things…"

and Macbeth's,

"Tomorrow, and tomorrow and tomorrow,
Creeps in it's petty pace from day to day…"

On the other hand we had to read Milton's "Paradise Lost" and "Paradise Regained." Although I had a genuine interest in the readings, I don't recall a single passage.

Remembering Father O'D's English Class…Father O'D had a sneaky way of teaching writing. In our junior year he would read from Poe and Twain. In our senior year, he began reading John Steinbeck's "The Red Pony," spreading the chapters over several weeks. It was Father O'D's way of saying, "listen carefully to these people's writing. Anyone can write well if they hear how good writers write."

Father's technique for grading composition was supportive of the student's efforts. He stated on the student's paper whether he thought the writing was strong or weak, and graded a marginal paper with two grades: "This is a C or B." He used praise not criticism to inspire better writing.

In mid-September 1953, while recovering from a knee injury suffered during the Junior-Senior football game, I was transferred from the Notre Dame Infirmary to St. Joseph's Hospital to have the knee drained.

The Post Card... I decided to design a post card on a piece of paper—even drew a two-cent stamp on the front right corner--and addressed it to his room, *"Father O'D, Headquarters, Sleepy Hollow."* My short note described the exciting moment at St. Joseph Hospital, when a Dr. Bodner and his nurse injected the knee with pontocaine to deaden the nerves, then withdrew several needles full (I said "needle fulls") of blood near the knee cap. I was surprised when Father O'D graded the paper post card: *"A or B"*, and returned it.

Father O'D's Vibrato... Since our sophomore year, several of us had sung at daily Masses celebrated by resident Priests, held in rooms outside the chapel. Often, we sang at Fr O'D's Mass. Father's singing became an unusual trill on high notes, giving new meaning to the word "vibrato." This was natural in his singing voice, not an affected or conscious effort on Father's part. We thought he lent beauty to the Mass with his vocal gift. I wished later that someone had recorded his singing voice. Father O'D would have made an impressive addition to the tenor section of our 4-part a cappella choir.

Father was a devout religious and would often pace outside Holy Cross House, reading his Office. On warm days it wasn't unusual to see him in his swim suit, alone on the St. Mary's pier, reading.

In his subtle way, Father O'D left his mark on each of us. In English class he provided a daily respite from the demands of our other classes.

Fr. Harold Riley, CSC

During my three years at Holy Cross, Father Harold "Hal" Riley was our superior. In some ways Father was an enigma, both a thinker and a doer, kind and benevolent, he possessed a touch of the little people in his almost indefinable, spontaneous nature. My final association with Father Riley changed my life forever.

Superior... I have the urge to say that Father Riley was the "Undisputed Superior of Holy Cross," since he appeared to us to possess an all prevailing drive to understand our needs and make things happen. I still picture him in his confessor stance, standing--in the hall, or the refectory or in his office--hands in his cassock pockets, head lowered, listening to another Priest or a visitor, or to one of us seminarians. In many ways Father Riley seemed more our resident chaplain than our superior.

Spontaneity... An example of Father's spontaneity is demonstrated in his approval of our junior class request to decorate the refectory for Halloween and allow a casket scene with a live corpse; and his last minute OK for a reading of Edgar Allan Poe's "The Tell-Tale Heart."

There were the many Holy Cross lawn parties—he called them *soirees*--where everyone developed a feeling of inclusion and welcome as part of the Holy Cross family. In one instance, he had Herman the grounds-keeper, a few Priests and several burly seniors dig a fire pit behind the new Butler building in order to roast ears of corn and potatoes for his most famous soiree.

The Change... During the summer vacation, following graduation from Holy Cross, most of the class spent the time with family and friends, preparing for their Novitiate year in Jordan, Minnesota, the Western Province Novitiate. It would be a year of contemplation, prayer and farm labor, and the acceptance of the temporary vows of poverty, chastity and obedience. There would be liturgical studies and related discussions but no college subjects taught during that year--a year's rest from a daily study regimen.

I was from Pittsburgh, Pennsylvania, and would be the only class member from Holy Cross to spend my Novitiate year at Bennington, Vermont, the Eastern Province Novitiate. For three years while at Holy Cross, I had played catch-up in studies and was tired of a study regimen. A novitiate year, free of studies, was a God send.

Just before graduation during our parents/student meetings, in Father Riley's office, Father explained that I would attend two years at Stonehill College in North Easton, Massachusetts before taking my Novitiate year.

I listened until Father completed his dictum, took a deep breath and explained my desire to attend novitiate year first, then justified my request by elaborating on my mental fatigue from playing catch up since joining Holy Cross in my sophomore year. I urged Father to consider sending me to my novitiate year, first.

Father listened patiently. In his kind and gentle way, Father lectured me on the soon-to-be-taken vow of obedience. I then mentioned the obvious, that all other Holy Cross seniors, my classmates, were Western Province and would attend Novitiate year that fall in Jordan Minnesota, before returning to their study regimen at Notre Dame. But, nothing more was discussed. Father talked cordially with the parents for a few minutes and we were dismissed. I wondered how many other meetings he would have with my classmates and their parents. Maybe some would not make it to Jordan, but would be dismissed following Holy Cross graduation.

As an aside, I had gone head-to-head with this giant personality, with my parents present, and my request was denied. Yet, I felt no embarrassment; no feeling at all of not winning. His quality of quiet, patient listening, careful response and friendly disagreement was, for me, Father Riley's defining moment. But I didn't give up.

After arriving home in Pittsburgh, I mailed a carefully prepared letter to Father Riley, again requesting that I be allowed to attend Novitiate year first, like the rest of my classmates, re-explaining my rationale. In a most pleasant response, Father Riley denied my request. I then formally declined the invitation to attend Stonehill College.

In later years, I often thought about my trips to visit two Holy Cross classmates' homes that summer. Were the trips a diversion, a way to avoid the pain of pondering the lost opportunity to complete my education and continue on with my vocation? I didn't allow myself the time to think about it. That fall, a close cousin and I joined the Navy.

Father Edward Shea, CSC

French Leçons... "VOgel, what did I just say?" There was a hard sound to the first syllable and an upswing on the final syllable. Vogel's name was delivered with a cynical, slightly nasal quality in Father Shea's baritone. It was our junior year, and first year French. Vogel was caught asleep at his desk.

Father Shea had a matter-of-fact delivery in class. There was no levity, no joke telling that I remember, just the facts, and only the facts. Still, Father was an experienced and wise teacher.

Natural Athlete... Father Shea was probably a typical Holy Cross Priest athlete, found not only at Notre Dame, but throughout the congregation of Holy Cross. We had heard that he played a formidable game of tennis. Like most stories about Holy Cross Priests, the story vs. the actual skill had to be tested. One example was Henry Reyes dare and the resulting foot race between Reyes and Father Larry LeVasseur. But it was a rare experience to see Father Shea on the playing fields or out of the classroom. I imagined his university teaching schedule was demanding.

In the fall of the following year, two teams of seniors had a pick-up basketball game on the outdoor half-courts, near St. Mary's lake. Father Shea walked by. He was most likely walking around the lake saying his Office prayers. Father offered to play for a few minutes. He was shorter than most of us. I thought he would be easy to guard. We seniors had played as a team many times before. Yet, it seemed impossible to guard or contain Father Shea. He made basket after basket—and he was wearing a cassock. We gained a new respect for Father Shea. He tolerated us.

Father Shea's Tolerance… "VOgel, give me the English translation of my sentence, and repeat it in French, please." Father Shea expected nothing from Vogel.

Vogel, red-faced from his sleep, appeared disoriented.

"Forgive me, Father, for I have sinned. Pardonnez-moi, mon pere, car j'ai peche."

The class burst into laughter. Vogel's response was perfectly correct.

"Father, I apologize for falling asleep, again." More laughter.

That was pure Vogel.

"Is that all you have to say? Vogel, you're useless. Go back to sleep. You seem to learn better that way." Father Shea tried valiantly to hide a smile.

Vogel was caught dozing off a few other times in Fr, Shea's class, but the amazing subconscious mind of the man always had the French translation. Looking back, Vogel was most fortunate to benefit from Father Shea's patience--and his tolerance.

Fr. William Simmons, CSC
Για την τιμή και δόξα του Θεού:
(Greek: "For the Honor and Glory of God")

We sometimes forget the influence a single individual can have on so many. Father Bill Simmons, a soft spoken Texan, was one of those individuals. He was brilliant with endless energy—a man of both character and class.

Staging Two Light Operas… During the 1954/55 school year, we Holy Cross seminarians were lucky to have Father Simmons, a resident Priest at Holy Cross, originally from the Notre Dame Department of Classics, to supervise and support the staging of "Oklahoma," and "H.M.S. Pinafore."

Because of the dual roles of men playing men and men playing women, Holy Cross's renditions of the light operas were comedies within comedies. Yet, both musicals had exceptional period costumes, a professional quality to the acting, and outstanding stage scenes, much of this thanks to Father Simmons.

The effort to produce the two light operas often became intense since, in addition to our class study demands, we had line memorization that required 100% mental application. Then, there were dancing classes in the movie hall, also known as "the Cave," located under the refectory where we ate our meals. And the effort expended on the dance routines and the fact that Father Simmons acted as one of the square dance directors often became hilarious. Once the routines were mastered, some of us continued to practice—the Promenade, the Allemande Right and Allemande Left, the Do-Si-Do--in the recreation room, in the classrooms before classes, and on the basketball court before, and sometimes during games.

Both musicals were staged to entertain our parents, the house Priests, and a few others from Notre Dame. But I'm sure that, during the preparation, we entertained ourselves far more than we ever entertained our guests.

It brings a smile of satisfaction just thinking of those two light operas, done up Holy Cross style. To many of us, the memories are right up there in importance with our four-part a capella choir, our team sports and anything else we accomplished during our years at Holy Cross.

Remembering Father Simmons' Greek Class...
Along with Father Brinker's Physics class, first year Greek was taught in our senior year at Holy Cross. Our course load also included fourth year English, advanced Latin and advanced French.

Father Simmons knew his Greek. He was able to follow the Greek primer's examples with examples of his own, and often provided additional insights, enhancing what he said with elaborate Greek-looking scratches on the chalk board. After the first few classes, Father most likely saw the terror in my eyes. He offered a consoling comment. Greek would be relatively easy. He assured us the Greek language wasn't nearly as difficult as Sanskrit, the Indian root language we'd begin to learn in our novitiate year.

I soon realized that not only was the Greek alphabet a hurdle, but the pronunciation was well beyond my limited Western Pennsylvanian English dialect. For several weeks into the semester, as I struggled with Greek, I mentioned my exasperation in the weekly letters home. Finally, oldest brother, Jack, came to my rescue in the form of a "cheat sheet." Typical of older brothers, Jack expected nothing in return, nor did he want to be bothered with my expressions of gratitude.

But a small packet of 35 vocabulary cards, measuring two-inches by four-inches, arrived in an unmarked business envelope. Each card contained eight English words with their Greek translations on the opposite side. Included with the cards was a note-book containing the translations for each exercise in the Greek 101 primer.

During that year, Father Simmons seemed more than pleased with my translations, and probably made some margin of allowance for my poor showing on exams.

Over the years I've misplaced the notebook of Greek 101 translations, possibly giving it to another struggling Greek scholar. Yet, for some reason lost to the ages, I still have the English/Greek vocabulary cards with my name, along with "AMDG." (Latin: "For the Honor and Glory of God") inscribed on the front card.

One day, during Greek class, Father Simmons noticed the AMDG on the cards and asked for the Greek translation. I submitted my Greek "versions" that he kindly returned without comment. Being a man of mercy, he let me off the hook, and provided the correct Greek translation on the returned sheet of paper.

While at Holy Cross, Father also taught advanced Latin. I think Kindness was among Father's greatest virtues, but always, first and foremost, he was a teacher. During a Holy Cross reunion at Notre Dame's Moreau House, it was mentioned that Father Simmons had been recovering from a serious cold. Several of our classmates walked across the lawn from Moreau to visit with Father, recuperating at Holy Cross (retirement) House. He appeared delighted to have the company. During the visit, Father's Latin class was mentioned in the conversation. One of the group, Jerry Wood, translated a Cicero Latin quote: "Dum Spiro, Spero" as "Where there's breath, there's hope." Father Simmons was coughing, but looked up immediately, and in his soft Texas drawl, corrected him,

"Jerry, it's 'While I breath, I hope.'" The group's laughter echoed down the halls of Holy Cross House.

Fr. John L. Van Wolvlear, C.S.C.

Punting... **F**ather's punt rose well above the mature trees that skirted the junior playing field. The football spiraled upward at a 45 degree angle. At its apex, the ball appeared to level out, parallel to the ground, float momentarily, then, its trajectory spent, plummet to the ground at the far end of the junior field, near St. Mary's Road.

Father Van Wolvlear--we called him Father Van--was a tall man, powerfully built through the shoulders and upper chest. Whether maneuvering on the playing field, or on the tennis court (before departing for the tennis courts, Father Van often commented: "I have a pastoral appointment at the court"), or simply walking down the main corridor at Holy Cross, Father Van's movements seemed more that of a cat's than of a large man.

Mutual Interests... As an aside, during my sophomore year, a friend and I conspired to work out each day for 30 minutes following sports activities, just before showering for evening chapel and dinner. We needed a place to work out. In short order we discovered the "cave," the movie auditorium beneath the refectory. At the far end of the auditorium a stage had been constructed some years earlier. Behind the stage a room had been built that was ideal for our work out.

We perfected a work-out routine. On alternate days, we performed 30 minutes of either upper or lower body exercises.

It was late in my senior year when I learned that Father Van and Father O'D performed daily exercises in their rooms or on campus, possibly at Rockne Hall. They said they were big on pushups, squats, side-straddle hops and running in place, each exercise a part of the exercise regimen my friend and I had followed in the cave.

Father picked up another football repeating perfectly his earlier kick, then another, and another. Punting a football was an occasional after-dinner sport for Father Van. Usually one or two of the resident Priests and a covey of students followed him down to the junior playing field. We would fan out at the far end of the field, hoping to retrieve and return footballs quickly enough for Father to continue repeating his inspiring kicks.

Father's punting exercise often happened immediately after dinner on warm, summer evenings. Normally, Father would be wearing his cassock. He'd hitch up one end and tuck it in his belt. His street shoes, sometimes tennis shoes, and dark slacks didn't impede him in any way. Every punt was a perfectly executed spiral, each football landing in a predictable pattern at the other end of the junior field.

The Unofficial Football Kicking Contest... Ed Doyle, a junior from Chicago, had a medium build. He may have weighed as much as 160 pounds; certainly no more. Doyle was a good athlete. He also had strong endurance, proven when he almost beat my brother, Norm, a senior, in a race up Tower Hill at Lake Michigan.

Doyle had just arrived on the field from the refectory. Father Van had kicked his final punt, watching it land while talking to Father O'D. As they turned to advance up the small rise of grass toward Holy Cross, the solid sound of a well kicked football made both Priests turn. The ball spiraled upward, flattened at its zenith and plunged to the ground. Both Priests were smiling and talking quietly to each other. Father Van finally said, "Mister Doyle, can you do that again?"

Doyle again executed a perfect spiral punt across the field toward St. Joe House. "Father, can you match that one?" Doyle derided, smiling.

"Mister Doyle must have eaten his Wheaties this morning. That was a very nice punt. Was it one of those smaller footballs or regulation size?"

Doyle laughed, grabbed one of the balls retrieved for Father Van and booted another punt as beautiful as the last.

Maybe Doyle realized he was a little off base challenging Father one-on-one. He quickly replied, "I'm working on distance, Father. Maybe some day I'll kick one as far as you."

"You're doing just fine, Mister Doyle. Keep up the good work and I'll see you the next time."

Doyle remained on the field kicking several perfect spirals, until the two Priests disappeared into the building. With each of Doyle's punts, Fathers Van and O'D glanced back to watch the spiraling ball arch upward and land at the far end of the junior field, near St. Mary's Road.

Father Van's appearance, even as he aged, was undeniably that of an athlete. While at Holy Cross, his persona was that of a calm and empathetic Priest who enjoyed his role as resident advisor, teacher and confessor.

THREE BROTHERS, C.S.C.

Brother Boniface, Brother Hormisdas and Brother Seraphim were known to many of us at Holy Cross Seminary (the Little Sem). All three Brothers were a presence at Notre Dame before, during, and after our departure from the university's Little Sem and Moreau senior seminary. In the early 1920's, when Brother Boniface and Brother Seraphim were young men, they arrived in America from Germany. They remained in each other's shadow for many years; initially as postulates in 1922, then while attending St. Joseph Novitiate in 1923, and when taking their final profession of vows in 1927. Brother Hormisdas' first profession of vows was also in1927, his final profession in 1930. All three Brothers had long tenures at the University of Notre Dame.

I'm sure that the three Brothers, though quiet participants, were dedicated Notre Damers, and appeared on the periphery of the many activities involving campus life. We seminarians frequently observed one or the other of the Brothers at Moreau seminary, or at Sacred Heart Church, or on the Little Sem grounds of Notre Dame.

Brother Boniface , C.S.C.

Brother Boniface, C.S.C (Titus Landenberger) was the Sacristan at Sacred Heart Church at Notre Dame for 38 years. Our Holy Cross Seminary a cappella, 4-part choir occasionally sang the Mass at Sacred Heart. We did not realize the many demands that went along with Brother's responsibility as sacristan. And yet he assumed additional duties, often beyond the scope of sacristan. He would be seen giving direction to the altar-boys--Notre Dame students whom he personally recruited and trained-- or adding final touches to the many altars and chapels at Sacred Heart and in the residence halls. Sacred Heart Church had numerous special occasions that brought many Priests to the University of Notre Dame. With a smile and super efficient administration, he handled the Masses and ceremonies seemingly without a show of stress or great effort.

Brother Boniface had a smile for everyone and was well liked by both students and faculty. A student newspaper article summed up his campus popularity, "Nobody around here is indispensable—unless it's Brother Boniface." Tom Hayes, a former Little Sem classmate, and our senior class president, commented that Brother had an outgoing personality. He was an extrovert by nature, sociable and friendly toward everyone—and admired for it. In the mid-1970's, Brother Boniface assumed his sacristan and other responsibilities at Notre Dame High School in Niles, Illinois. I had been long gone from Notre Dame and the Little Sem, raising a young family in Virginia.

Yet, on a visit to Pittsburgh, Father Pete Sandonato, CSC, a fellow Pittsburgher and the religious superior of Notre Dame High School, commented to his parents regarding Brother Boniface's rapport with everyone. Later, Father Eugene Burke, successor to Father Sandonato, who knew Brother for over 30 years, commented on Brother Boniface's ability to relate to persons of any age, from children to young high school students, to adults and to persons of his own age. At the time, Brother Boniface was in his late 70s!

Bro. Hormisdas, C.S.C.

Jim Callahan, a fellow classmate and my senior year Little Sem roommate commented with incredulity "He could draw a perfectly straight line with a paint brush!" Brother Hormisdas, C.S.C. (Jacob Joseph Spanier) was an artist who loved to paint. Often he could be heard whistling quietly while he painted. He performed other maintenance functions as well, trained in carpentry, construction and tool and machine repair. During his nearly 40 year tenure, he travelled within the Holy Cross Congregation to six States and to Europe (Holy Cross parish in Czartorysk, Poland), performing his maintenance services in extreme cold and primitive living conditions—he later said he enjoyed it! It's been told that Brother painted every square inch of the Little Sem— some areas more than once.

While in my senior year at the Little Sem, I was assigned the task of Priest waiter and often saw Brother

Hormisdas at breakfast, lunch and supper. This was part of his seminary philosophy. To help bolster morale at the Little Sem, Brother felt that, like other resident staff, we seminarians expected him to attend the meals, soirees, the movie nights, chapel meditations and Mass celebrations.

Brother Hormisdas's faith was one of his strongest virtues. He once commented that Faith is a lit candle in the hand, giving enough light for one step. "Take that one step and you have light enough for the next step."

Brother Hormisdas' life purpose was to do the will of God. The word "YES!" he explained was his favorite prayer. He was dedicated to faithfully fulfilling this prayer, often whispering it to himself and later sharing his prayer with the other religious at the Little Sem.

It does not seem that long ago that we seminarians had the unparalleled experience of spending our formative years living among the Brothers, resident Priests and Sisters at the University of Notre Dame's Holy Cross and Moreau Seminaries. We were blessed early on with walking examples of the exemplary life; and in their own quiet way, the religious shaped the character of each of us. This has served us well throughout our lives.

Brother Seraphim, C.S.C.

While we attended our classes, Brother Seraphim, C.S.C. (Edward Herrmann) devoted most of his 11 year tenure at Notre Dame to landscaping the grounds at Moreau Senior Seminary, doing large scale gardening, or planting trees— sometimes cutting them down--and caring for the large vegetable gardens and a few acre melon patch near St. Mary's Road.

On our return to the Little Sem in the late summer of 1952, we seminarians felt obligated to taste the melons. Many disappeared along the border of the patch on St. Mary's road. I'm sure we had some concern that Brother had observed us, sneaking through the senior playing field and across St. Mary's road to gorge ourselves on the fruits of Brother's labors.

As an aside, in 1966, on a visit with my wife and two children to the Little Sem, I visited with Father Fiedler. Apparently, Father had heard the rumor that my sophomore class had stolen melons from Brother Seraphim's melon patch a dozen years earlier. Smiling, he asked if there was any credence to the rumor. I said that I had heard the same rumor. We both laughed. It was shortly after that I discovered Brother Seraphim was still at Notre Dame, preparing to leave Moreau for Holy Cross House where he performed landscaping and gardening for another 20 years.

Brother Seraphim's landscaping efforts at Moreau produced works of art and beauty. He had an obvious green thumb and, while we were at the Little Sem, we feasted on the many varieties of harvested vegetables and fruits—home-grown food-- not only grown and harvested for our community tables, but also for many tables of the poor in the area.

Jerry Wood or Tom Hayes commented that Brother Seraphim was a sour puss, and then quickly added that Brother had a good heart. Father Len Banas elaborated, describing Brother as having a somewhat "crusty" exterior; but behind that first glance was a remarkable sense of humor, great kindness, urbanity and sensitivity to the finer things in life. "Brother had a great love of opera and good music." Father Banas should know Brother Seraphim well. On Father's several hour trips to Chicago and back, he would offer Brother Seraphim a ride to visit with the Brother's niece or nephew.

THREE SISTERS OF NOTRE DAME

Through the late 1960's, Holy Cross Seminary, housed in a large Victorian building, located on the campus of the University of Notre Dame, housed 200 young aspirants to the Priesthood, a dozen or more resident teaching-Priest-faculty and three Sisters of Notre Dame. The Sisters occupied private quarters, located on the southwest corner of Holy Cross, overlooking St. Mary's Lake..The Sisters served meals seven days a week to the resident Priests and to a few hundred of us young seminarians. One of the Sisters was a nurse and, administered daily medical assistance to us young men. I've heard that the Sisters were occasionally approached by a homesick, dispirited or discouraged seminarian, needing an assurance that they belonged at Holy Cross.

As a young seminarian, I was most fortunate to know these three Sisters of Notre Dame. Two of the Sisters, **Sister Mary Zacharia Bahman** and **Sister Mary Amata Döring**, managed the kitchen at Holy Cross. Sister Zacharia, endowed with high energy and a good heart, was recognized as the undisputed spokesperson of the kitchen. Sister "Zack", as we often referred to her--outside of ear shot of course, directed the pantry and kitchen operations. Sister Amata, the chief cook, also an industrious soul, spoke little but listened thoughtfully and had a ready smile for everyone. Sister often prayed as she performed the daily cooking tasks, pronouncing the words quietly to herself. Many of us viewed Sister Amata as a living saint. **Sister Mary St. Rita Petkosh** had immeasurable compassion and a talent for diagnosis and healing. Sister managed the Holy Cross dispensary and infirmary.

The Sisters as well as the resident teaching Priests and Brothers at Holy Cross were benevolent by nature. Daily, we students were exposed to individuals "Living the Faith," and demonstrating exactly what the term meant in both the Catholic and Notre Dame traditions.

Some years after graduating from Holy Cross, I wrote a series of abstracts on what life was like at the seminary. More recently, the abstracts became a few hundred page book (PREP SCHOOL DAYS, *The Seminary at the University of Notre Dame*). From this book and from several Holy Cross classmates, I obtained some treasured memories of our Sisters of Notre Dame.

Sister Mary Amata, SND

Sister Amata had wonderful communication skills. Though her spoken English was poor, Sister understood English well and listened to everyone, offering a short statement, a nod and her ever-present smile. When Sister Zacharia monitored the daily cleaning of dish-washing equipment, or the cleaning of the large nickel stove or the pots and pans, Sister Amata would oversee as well, but Sister always seemed to disappear from the kitchen before Sister Zacharia, to attend their evening prayers in the Sisters' chapel.

Few of us knew that Sister Amata had trained as a nurse's aide in Germany. Her mother was a registered nurse and they worked in a hospital run by the Franciscan Sisters. She became ill with what, at the time, was diagnosed as tuberculosis. Her lifelong dream of becoming a Sister-nurse slipped away. Yet, while in Germany, Sister Amata had honed her cooking skill to the point where, following her novice training at the Sisters of Notre Dame, she received the white

75

habit of a Sister-cook. Sister Amata was the chief cook at Holy Cross Seminary for 11 years.

Sauerkraut... No one knew until hours before a meal when Sisters Amata and Zacharia's home-made sauerkraut would be served. During preparation and following dinner, the aroma filled the house. It was a delicious treat that contributed to us seminarians gaining many pounds during our stay at Holy Cross. Unfortunately, the secret of its unique preparation was most likely lost to the ages when Holy Cross Seminary closed its doors in 1967.

Bread Pudding... We boys never made a fuss when Sister Amata's bread pudding (a.k.a. lead pudding) was served at dinner. To the best of recollection, the recipe included broken-up bread pieces, warm milk, eggs, and sugar--and possibly melted butter, raisins, vanilla, and molasses. After baking, Sister added a topping of fresh grape jelly. Sister Zacharia most likely assisted Sister Amata with her bread pudding creation. Being uncomplaining young men, we ate what was placed in front of us. Yet, for a few of those among us, Sister's bread pudding was their undoing.

For example, it only recently has come to light that several finicky eaters, all former Holy Cross classmates, admitted they had, over the years, been offered the tempting treat of bread pudding, only to remember Holy Cross style bread pudding. Yet, it's been reported that most of the complainers have repented, giving in to the temptation to try bread pudding. Now, the tasty treat has become their favorite dessert! Psychologists may call the change of heart *transference*, but I personally feel the credit for this latter-day miracle must be attributed to Blessed Sister Amata.

Mystery Squares…Some of these individuals also blamed… er, credited Sister Amata with "mystery Squares," a well received item that appeared on Fridays. According to one classmate, back in the day, these breaded and possibly deep fried treats mimicked bread pudding and "are not found on any restaurant menu." Of course, we rush to Sr. Amata's defense, remembering the daily pots of down-home coffee, served with the cream already added and, on Feast Days, the meals of steak, green beans, mashed potatoes, gravy--and bread pudding.

Sister Mary St. Rita, SND

The **Dispensary...** The Holy Cross dispensary fell under the jurisdiction of Sister St. Rita. Sister was a scant five-feet tall, tiny to us growing young men. She maintained a pleasant but firm disposition.

What Sister St. Rita managed to do so well, probably without being aware of it, was to provide us a place of refuge, away from the playing field, away from the discipline and house obediences (assigned tasks), and away from the study regimen at Holy Cross.

If we had a sore throat, a cut or abrasion, or suffered any ache or pain, then, following final chapel in the evening, we were expected to go to the dispensary. Sister St. Rita addressed a long line of complainants each evening. I was one of them.

"Next in line, please."

At least several dozen times during my three years at Holy Cross, Sister swabbed a sore throat with sweet methiolate, or disinfected a cut or abrasion with Mercurochrome or a dab of anti-biotic cream and a patch.

The dispensary, a twelve by six foot room, was meticulous. The painted floor always looked freshly cleaned. Sister's medicines and supplies were stored in a white cabinet with a glass front. In addition, a small table held an open bottle of sweet methiolate, and a clear glass bottle filled with cotton balls. Next to the glass bottle stood a stainless steel container holding a large supply of swabs. The room also contained a study hall chair where you sat if Sister decided to bandage a larger wound or to give an injection.

It seemed that most of us were there with sore throats, so received the throat swab remedy. Often, one of us would require a band aid or larger gauze pad for a scratch or cut. These simple first aid solutions were administered as we stood just outside the dispensary door.

"Next in line, please," became Sister St. Rita's rallying cry to the student body.

I remember Ed LeMasse, a tough hided senior from Chicago, holding up the line for at least 20 minutes. Sister wanted to administer a needle into his lower right arm. LeMasse, a quick and wiry competitor on the playing field, was sitting down, resting his elbow on the study hall chair, his arm bent. Every time Sister attempted to push in the needle, it broke. Sister smiled, determined, and produced a larger needle. After several tries Sister had success. LeMasse left the dispensary red faced and shaken.

Early in my junior year, I was sitting in study hall after a particularly competitive football game. During the game, I had caught several long passes and performed kick-offs. Following the game I felt beat but pushed myself to do a lap around St. Mary's Lake.

It came on fast, the old rheumatic pains in my knees that I had experienced during a lost summer with rheumatic fever, following my fifth grade. Shortly, I was unable to tolerate the aching and went to the Sisters' quarters asking for Sister St. Rita. Sister listened quietly, and asked me to wait in the nuns' guest room. Upon her return she had a large glass of cold water and a small paper envelope containing a dozen or so pills. Sister called them APCs.

"Take three now, and two with a full glass of water every four hours—and no football or excessive running tomorrow. I'll see you at the dispensary this evening and tomorrow evening."

I was ushered out of the Sisters' quarters.

In my estimation, the APCs were a miracle drug. Shortly after taking the pills, there was absolutely no knee pain. It would be a few years later that I rediscovered APCs in the Navy. They were a combination of Aspirin, Phenacetin, and Caffeine, a reliable pain killer similar to, but in my experience more effective and quicker acting, than Excedrin.

Some years after graduating from Holy Cross, following a stint in the Navy, marriage and raising three children, my only daughter attended Notre Dame Academy in Middleburg, VA. On her first day at the academy, who came to greet my wife and family but Sister St. Rita. One of the first remarks Sister made was that I visited the dispensary too much at Holy Cross.

"I think that was my brother, Jack, Sister. We look alike," I blurted out, surprised at Sister's recall.

"No, it was you Andrew. Your brother Norman introduced you when you first came to the seminary."

How do you fight a statement like that? I didn't remember being introduced by Norm, but I decided this was one of those lose-lose situations. I shut up, and Sister continued on,

"You and Mr. Zahradnik were my noisiest patients when you both were sick in the infirmary."

I smiled, realizing that I would have to tell someone that story some day.

Remembering the Infirmary… During the spring of my junior year, I caught a flu-like bug. Up to Sister St. Rita's dispensary I went, weak and fevered.

"You'll have to move to the infirmary for a few days." Sister said.

I retrieved my bathrobe and slippers and shaving kit, and then reported to the dispensary. Sister led me to the infirmary. She opened the door and allowed me to enter, pointing me toward a bed. I discovered that a senior, Ray Zahradnik, had also been admitted to the infirmary.

Zahradnik was also from Pennsylvania. A year earlier, he was a sophomore monitor. Many times he had helped me solve geometry problems in the hall mop closet outside the study hall. He was far beyond most in the classroom, and appeared to be a natural athlete on the playing field.

Apparently we both suffered from the same symptoms.

"You look pretty sick," he managed to say, smiling, tucked in under several layers of sheets and blankets. I was shivering and unable to do other than greet Zahradnik with a mumble. I remember nothing more until the following morning. Zahradnik was sitting on the side of his bed, holding his head.

"Don't worry about the fever and shakes, that's short-lived. The headache and coughing are the killers." He attempted a laugh, ending up with a hacking cough.

"Sister St. Rita will heal us with one of her miracle cures," I managed to respond, lost in my own pain and misery.

Later in the day, we both felt somewhat better, but concluded that we'd been placed in quarantine. We decided to make the best of it.

Sister St. Rita monitored our meals and, at least once, commented on our behavior—our laughing and talking too loud. We apologized with promises to "keep it down."

Each day we had meals delivered from the kitchen with Sister overseeing the food served. We suffered hacking coughs and minor breathing problems. Sister checked up on us several times each day, taking vital signs.

Zahradnik left the dispensary a day before I did.

"How do you plan to catch up on studies?" I asked,

always concerned about what I had missed in classes. Zahradnik laughed, and after a short fit of coughing and clearing his throat responded.

"I plan to go to the recreation room during the afternoon break and read physics. That's the only one I'll have to catch up on. The rest are easy."

Sister discharged me the following day, in time for lunch. Following lunch, I short cut through the senior recreation room to attend a class at the new Butler building, next door. Sure enough, there was Zahradnik, lounging in an easy chair, reading through his physics book and carrying on a conversation with a classmate. Later, I asked how the difficult subjects came to him so easily. He smiled,

"I think it's my IQ. I'm told it's 180."

I think Sister St. Rita's medicine saved the life of a natural athlete and brilliant scholar. She also saved mine.

Anyone who met Sister St. Rita would not easily forget her kind and giving nature. Tom Hayes, our Holy Cross senior class president, had an expression for stellar humans. He referred to them as "Archangels." That perfectly describes Sister St. Rita.

Sr. Mary Zacharia, SND

Visiting Sundays... Parents' Visiting Sundays at Holy Cross were scheduled monthly, through the fall and spring. My family visited once in the fall and once in the spring. My mother would always ask to visit with Sister Zacharia and Sister Amata. As mentioned, both Sisters were cooks for Holy Cross House. Their ability to deliver daily satisfying meals to a few hundred people, a majority comprised of growing, hungry young men, was awe inspiring.

The War... During one visit, I remember mom and Sister Zacharia entertaining each other for some time with stories of growing up, mom in a small college town in Pennsylvania and Sister Zacharia in a small town in Germany. Sister Amata sat quietly, smiling. She comprehended everything and added only short comments from time to time, due to her limited ability to speak English.

Sister Zacharia and my mother spoke at length about the war years. Mom had lost her only brother, a marine aviator, in the Pacific. I recall one dark story that Sister Zacharia related of her and Sister Amata's families' plights in Germany during the World War, the forced labor, the fighting, and the families' suffering and deaths. Two of Sister Amata's Sisters suffered in concentration camps, and two of her brothers gave their lives in the war. But mom and the Sisters were strong individuals, able to handle the pain of relating these sad memories without breaking down

Budgie Bird... My mother and Sister Zacharia were not morbid people; quite the opposite. Mom always inquired about Sister's parakeet. For some time they would fawn over "Budgie bird." I experienced a relaxed, happier side to Sister Zacharia.

Those of us working the dishwasher or having obedience assignments in other parts of the kitchen were expected to do exactly as Sister Zacharia requested. If you demonstrated cooperation and were hard working, she referred to you as Hans ("Hanz"), an almost sacred title with Sister Zacharia. Before I was assigned to kitchen duty, I had heard the rumor that, if you landed on Sister's bad side, you suffered the terrible penance of being labeled "Fritz," almost forever. In fairness to Sister Zacharia, I should mention that I had a habit of transferring the stern natures of the Sisters of Charity, back home, onto Sister Zacharia and the other Sisters at Holy Cross. I was always on guard.

The Milk Dispenser Incident... But, thinking back, maybe I did make a few points with Sister Zacharia. During the parent's final visit before my graduation, I related a kitchen incident to mom and dad. Recently, as a new obedience (daily house assignment), I had been placed in charge of the dishwasher operation. As a senior with three years of year-round sports, I was probably in the best physical condition while at Holy Cross.

One of my kitchen duties was to load two five-gallon milk containers into a milk dispenser that stood several feet off the floor. As I reached down and began to lift one of the five gallon containers, Sister Zacharia appeared out of nowhere.

"Here, Hanz, let me do that. You'll hurt your self." Sister easily lifted the first five-gallon container with one hand, shifting it into place in the dispenser. She quickly lifted the second five gallon container, juggled it into position next to the first, then disappeared back into the pantry. I stood quietly for a moment, admiring what I'd just seen and trying not to laugh over the whole thing.

I can safely say that without the positive influence of the Sisters of Notre Dame at Holy Cross, all of us boys would have been a lot poorer and most likely a lot thinner for the experience.

The Grease Trap... I recall a late afternoon, on a weekend, when several of my classmates and I had returned to Holy Cross from Washington Hall, after attending a Notre Dame students' stage play Serendipity. We hummed show tunes, laughed about some of the scenes and discussed the professionalism of the actors. It was an enjoyable play and a welcome break from the strict regimen of life at Holy Cross. We decided to walk through the dishwasher room, and down a side hall to see what was going on in the senior recreation room.

I had recently been given a new daily assignment in the kitchen. After each meal, I monitored the soap levels and water heat levels as three classmates and I fed several hundred dishes, bowls, cups and silverware into the 30 foot long, stainless steel behemoth.

Sister Zacharia appeared from the kitchen cooking area, smiling, beckoning to me. I should have sensed trouble and been on guard.

"How queasy is your stomach, Hanz?"
Sister Zacharia smiled again. She carried a long spoon-like metal rod and a small shovel. Her large frame blocked the sun reflecting off the stainless steel dishwasher, the rays absorbed into Sister's white robes.

"Sister, I don't think I have a queasy stomach."
"Good, follow me."

It was a direct order. I obediently followed Sister. She walked around the perimeter of the dishwasher, and out the side door into the cool spring evening. Sister pointed to a door and a short set of stairs, located near the entrance to the Sister's quarters. I followed her into a small cellar that ended at a wall directly beneath the dish washing room, above.

"See the plate in the floor? Here, I show you how to do this. Watch how I open the grease-trap."

Sister was huffing and puffing as she leaned over with the long metal rod, and inserted it into an 18 inch metal plate built into the basement floor. With a single twist of her wrist, the plate came loose. The smell from old grease and other putrification that arose from the hole made me catch my breath.

"I'll let you clean it out, Hanz. Bring over an empty coffee can."

Sister pointed toward some empty, several gallon coffee cans stacked against the basement wall.

"You clean by pulling up the trap slowly and emptying the old grease into a coffee can. Also, use this small shovel to clean anything remaining in the bottom, or the sludge will back up into the kitchen dishwasher. It must be done every Saturday."

"I understand Sister."

I cleaned the grease trap quickly, and picked up the half full coffee can.

"You put the collected grease next to the dumpster, on the side of the steam house. It is picked up each week."

"Yes Sister, OK."

I was anxious to get rid of the can as quickly as possible.

Upon returning from the dumpster, Sister Zacharia was standing outside the kitchen door.

"Very good, Hanzie; come, I show you where to put the tools."

I followed Sister back into the kitchen.

"Every Saturday morning, Hanz; and tomorrow, I show you how to clean the cook stove with a brush."
Sister disappeared through the kitchen, into the Sister's quarters.

I continued on my way to the recreation room. I wondered what I would tell my classmates to explain the smell on my clothes, and the meeting with Sister Zacharia. I tried to get my mind off the grease-trap's sludge smell by humming one of the show tunes from "Serendipity."

It was just another day; started out the same old way...
I felt queasy in the stomach and realized it wasn't just another day.

Three Sister of Notre Dame

After contacting many former Holy Cross classmates, requesting their reflections on and recollections of the Sisters of Notre Dame at Holy Cross, there appears to be little deviation in our expressed sentiments for the Sisters. We cared about them, and admired and respected them. There is no question in our minds why these three unforgettable holy women heeded the call to be Sisters of Notre Dame.

ACKNOWLEDGEMENTS

Many of the stories herein (some modified and/or added to), are mentioned in "PREP SCHOOL DAYS, *The Seminary at the University of Notre Dame.*"

For their on-going interest, my thanks once again to **Fr. Len Banas, Fr. Bill Brinker, Fr. Tom Blantz** and **Fr. Bill Simmons,** as well as former classmates **Jim Callahan, Tom Hayes, Jim Keating** and **Jerry Wood.** In addition, other former classmates who offered anecdotes and comments on "Some Notre Dame Greats I've Known," are **Jim Bradley, Dave Jecman, Bob Kuker** and **Ted Ricks.**

For their interest, help and support, I thank and applaud **Deb Buzzard**, at Notre Dame's Holy Cross Province archives, and two Sisters of Notre Dame: **Sister Mary Joan Terese Niklas** at the Covington, KY Province, and **Sister Mary Elizabeth Wood** at the Chardon, OH Province.

HOLY CROSS SEMINARY AT THE UNIVERSITY OF NOTRE DAME: CLASS OF 1955

CLASS MOTTO: *"What is taught we learn; what may be found we seek; what may be prayed for we ask of God."*

BACK: Norm Lakatos, Jon Lullo, Jim Keating*, Rog Sowala*, Mike Gelven, Dave Gibson*, Jim Callahan*, Tom Norris*, Dick Cavanaugh, Jude McCusker*, Ron Vogel*, Don Kaiser*

FRONT: Andy Stevans, Lee Skinner*, Bob Kuker*, Jerry Wood*, Tom Hayes*, Fr. Leonard Banas, Fr. Larry LeVasseur, Fr. Harold Riley, Fr. Dean O'Donnell, Don Parks, Jim Glaza, Dick Howard, Ed Whelan*

NOTE: Many Holy Cross graduates including many of the class of 1955 (*) are also graduates of the University of Notre Dame.